FRONTISPIECE. Urbino. Ceiling painting, Ducal Palace, XVI cent.
[*Farbige Decorationen*]

RENAISSANCE AND BAROQUE

Ceiling Masterpieces

DOVER PUBLICATIONS, INC.
MINEOLA, NEW YORK

Bibliographical Note

This Dover edition, first published in 2008, is an original selection of 75 plates from the following sources: *Farbige Decorationen,* edited by Ernst Ewald and published by E. Wasmuth, Berlin, 1889–1896, and *La Peinture Décorative en France du xvi au xviii siècle,* edited by Lafille and Gelis-Didot and published by Schmidt, Paris, in 1880.

DOVER *Pictorial Archive* SERIES

Library of Congress Cataloging-in-Publication Data

Renaissance and Baroque ceiling masterpieces.
     p. cm. — (Dover pictorial archive series)
  Original selection of 75 plates from Farbige Decorationen, edited by Ernst Ewald and published by E. Wasmuth, Berlin, 1889–1896, and La peinture décorative en France du xvi au xviii siècle, edited by Lafille and Gelis-Didot and published by Schmidt, Paris, in 1880.
  ISBN-13: 978-0-486-46529-6
  ISBN-10: 0-486-46529-2
  1. Mural painting and decoration, Renaissance. 2. Mural painting and decoration, Baroque. 3. Decoration and ornament, Renaissance. 4. Decoration and ornament, Baroque. I. Dover Publications, Inc.

ND2725.R46 2008
751.7—dc22

2008005290

Manufactured in the United States of America
Dover Publications, Inc., 31 East 2nd Street, Mineola, N.Y. 11501

Publisher's Note

It is not often that a ceiling is the backdrop for a splendidly executed painting, but, during the Renaissance and Baroque periods, many of the premier artists of the day applied their talents to decorating the view above. The most famous example of ceiling painting is, of course, that of the Sistine Chapel, a vast space that was painstakingly decorated in fresco by Michelangelo over a period of years. Many other artists, such as Veronese, Tintoretto, Fragonard, Titian, Mantegna, and Salviati, produced notable ceiling paintings. The spaces utilized were churches and castles, as well as privately owned buildings and public areas. For example, Plate 24 shows a ceiling painting from the residence of Isabella d'Este in the Ducal Palace in Mantua; Plate 42 reproduces the painting from a ceiling in the Uffizi Gallery, Florence; and Plate 69 depicts a ceiling in the Parc de Petit-Trianon, Versailles. The striking collection of color plates also includes ceilings from palaces, government buildings, and hotels. The Vatican is represented with a view of a ceiling in the Borgia apartments.

Ranging from Italy and Germany to France, Bohemia, and Tunisia, the styles and subject matter of the Renaissance, Renaissance-style, and Baroque ceiling paintings in this volume are consistently interesting and varied. Reflecting the notion of the "rebirth" of culture after the Middle Ages, the Renaissance (the mid-fourteenth through the sixteenth centuries) was characterized by an appreciation of the Classical art and literature of ancient Greece and Rome. These elements form the subject matter of many of the ceiling paintings in this book, with references to mythological figures and themes. The Baroque period (the sixteenth through eighteenth centuries), which followed the Renaissance, introduced ornamentation and decoration for its own sake into European art and architecture of the time. The balanced values of Renaissance art can be contrasted with the more energetically ornate approach of Baroque expression. The courts of Louis XIV and Louis XV are especially associated with the extravagances of Baroque style in the decorative arts.

The seventy-five color plates presented in *Renaissance and Baroque Ceiling Masterpieces* have been selected from two rare nineteenth-century portfolios: *Farbige Decorationen,* edited by Ernst Ewald and published by E. Wasmuth, Berlin, in 1889 to 1896; and *La Peinture Décorative en France du xvi au xviii siècle,* edited by Laffille and Gelis-Didot and published by Schmidt, Paris, in 1880. The captions accompanying the plates indicate the geographic location of the ceiling painting portrayed in each single plate or double-page spread, as well as pertinent information (e.g., "vaulted ceiling") where available, and the date it was painted ("n.d." indicates that no date is given in the source). Each caption also specifies which of the two sources was used for the color plate.

PLATE 1. Berlin. Ceiling painting, department store, Friedrichstrasse 77, n.d.
[*Farbige Decorationen*]

PLATE 2. Rome. Frieze and ceiling painting. Kloster der Penitenzieri, XVI cent.
[*Farbige Decorationen*]

PLATE 3. Rome. Vaulted ceiling decoration, Kloster der Penitenzieri, XVI cent.
[*Farbige Decorationen*]

PLATE 4. Bohemia. Ceiling painting, Neuhaus Castle, XVI cent.
[*Farbige Decorationen*]

PLATE 5. Bohemia. Ceiling painting, Neuhaus Castle, XVI cent.
[*Farbige Decorationen*]

PLATES 6–7. Versailles. Ceiling painting, government office, Court of Louis XIV, n.d.
[*Farbige Decorationen*]

PLATE 8. Florence. Ceiling painting, Uffizi Gallery, XVI cent.
[*Farbige Decorationen*]

PLATE 9. Prague. Ceiling painting, Town Hall, XVII cent.
[*Farbige Decorationen*]

PLATE 10. Rome. Ceiling painting. Kloster der Penitenzieri, XVI cent.
[*Farbige Decorationen*]

PLATE 11. Berlin. Ceiling painting, n.d.
[*Farbige Decorationen*]

PLATE 12. Genoa. Ceiling painting by Pierin del Vaga, Palace of Andrea Doria, XVI cent.
[*Farbige Decorationen*]

PLATE 13. Genoa. Vaulted ceiling. Palace of Andrea Doria, XVI cent.
[Farbige Decorationen]

PLATES 14–15. Mantua. Ceiling painting, Ducal Palace, Appartamento dei Stivali, XVI cent.
[*Farbige Decorationen*]

PLATE 16. Rome. Ceiling painting, Palazzo della Cancelleria, XVI cent.
[*Farbige Decorationen*]

PLATE 17. Rome. Ceiling painting, Palazzo della Cancelleria, XVI cent.
[*Farbige Decorationen*]

PLATES 18–19. Parma. Ceiling painting, cathedral nave, XVI cent.
[*Farbige Decorationen*]

PLATES 20–21. Munich. Ceiling painting, n.d.
[*Farbige Decorationen*]

PLATE 22. Berlin. Ceiling painting, billiard hall, n.d.
[*Farbige Decorationen*]

PLATE 23. Magdeburg. Ceiling painting, n.d.
[*Farbige Decorationen*]

PLATE 24. Mantua. Ceiling painting, Ducal Palace; residence of Isabella d'Este, n.d.
[*Farbige Decorationen*]

PLATE 25. Pompeii. Ceiling painting, Casa del Gallo, n.d.
[*Farbige Decorationen*]

Plates 26–27. Augsburg. Ceiling painting, great bathing area in Fuggerhause, XVII cent.
[*Farbige Decorationen*]

PLATE 28. Mantua. Ceiling painting, Ducal Palace, XVI cent.
[*Farbige Decorationen*]

PLATE 29. Padua. Ceiling painting, Scuola del Santo, XVI cent.
[*Farbige Decorationen*]

PLATES 30–31. Mantua. Fresco by Mantegna, Castello di Corte, Camera degli Sposi, XV cent.
[*Farbige Decorationen*]

PLATES 32–33. Rome. Ceiling painting, Vatican, Borgia apartments. XV cent.
[*Farbige Decorationen*]

PLATE 34. Rome. Ceiling painting, Basilica of Santa Maria sopra Minerva, XVI cent.
[*Farbige Decorationen*]

PLATE 35. Rome. Ceiling painting, Scrofa-Calcagnini Palace, XVI cent.
[*Farbige Decorationen*]

PLATES 36–37. Rome. Ceiling painting. Villa di Papa Giulio, XVI cent.
[*Farbige Decorationen*]

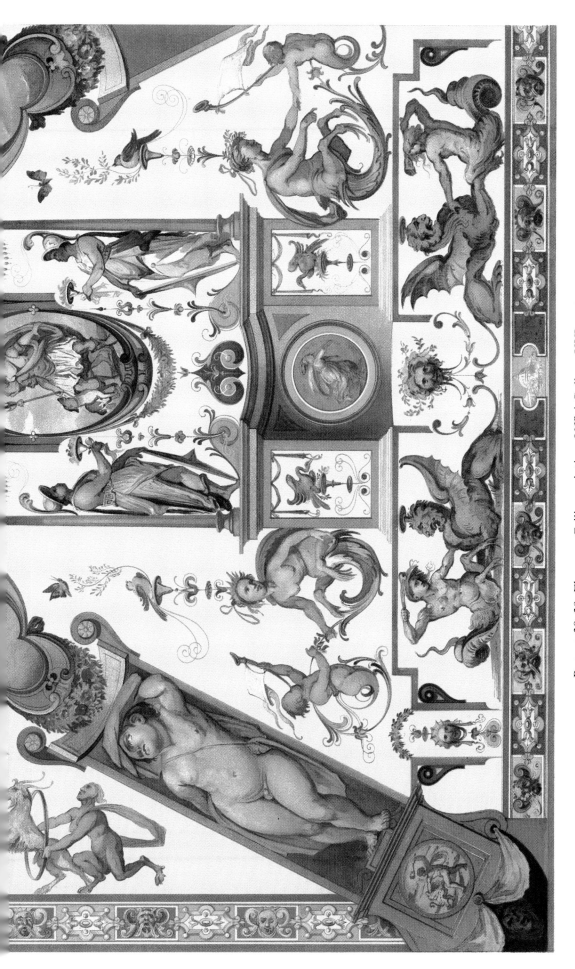

PLATES 38–39. Florence. Ceiling painting. Uffizi Gallery. XVI cent.
[*Farbige Decorationen*]

PLATES 40–41. Florence. Ceiling painting, Uffizi Gallery, XVI cent.
[*Farbige Decorationen*]

PLATE 42. Florence. Ceiling painting, Uffizi Gallery, XVI cent.
[*Farbige Decorationen*]

PLATE 43. Milan. Ceiling painting, S. Maurizio, XVI cent.
[*Farbige Decorationen*]

PLATE 44. Berlin. Ceiling painting, banquet hall in former palace, XVIII cent.
[*Farbige Decorationen*]

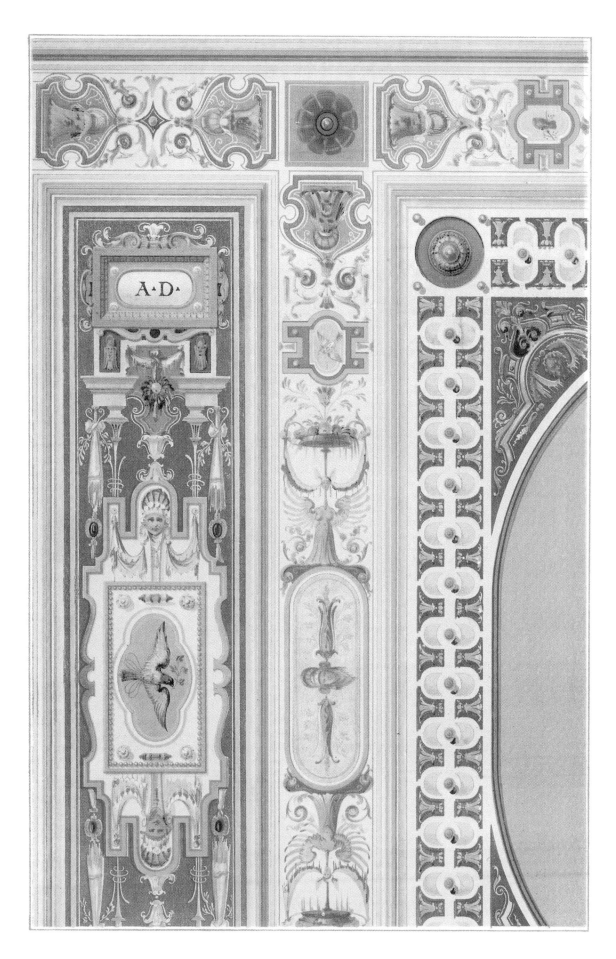

PLATE 45. Landshut. Ceiling painting, Knights' Hall, Trausnitz Castle, XVI cent.
[*Farbige Decorationen*]

PLATES 46–47. Mantua. Ceiling painting, Ducal Palace, Appartamento dei Stivali, XVI cent.
[*Farbige Decorationen*]

PLATES 48–49. Tunis. Ceiling painting, Bardo Palace, n.d.
[*Farbige Decorationen*]

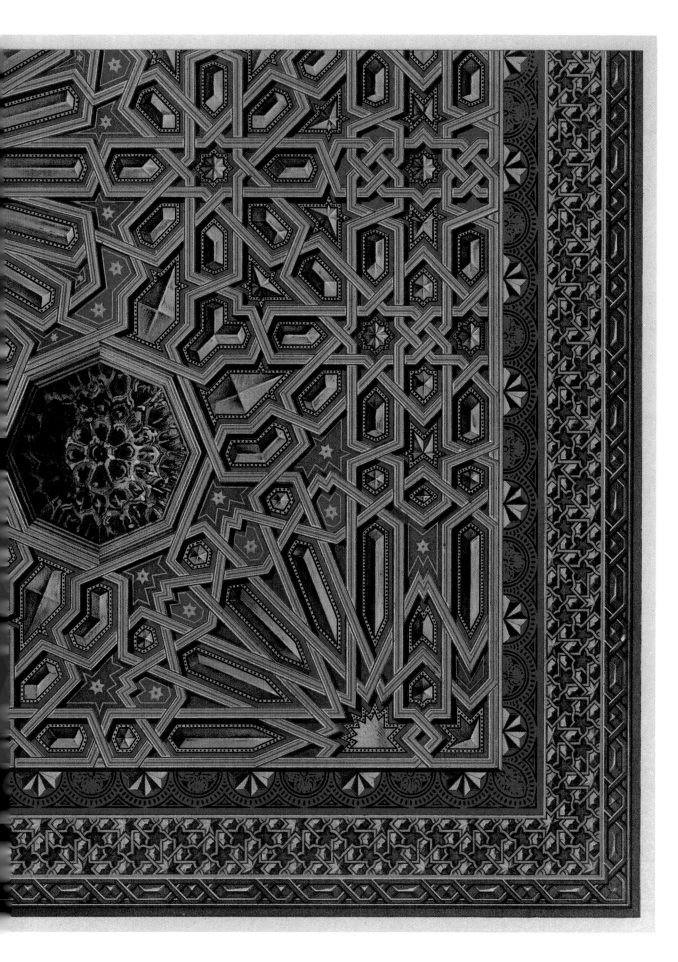

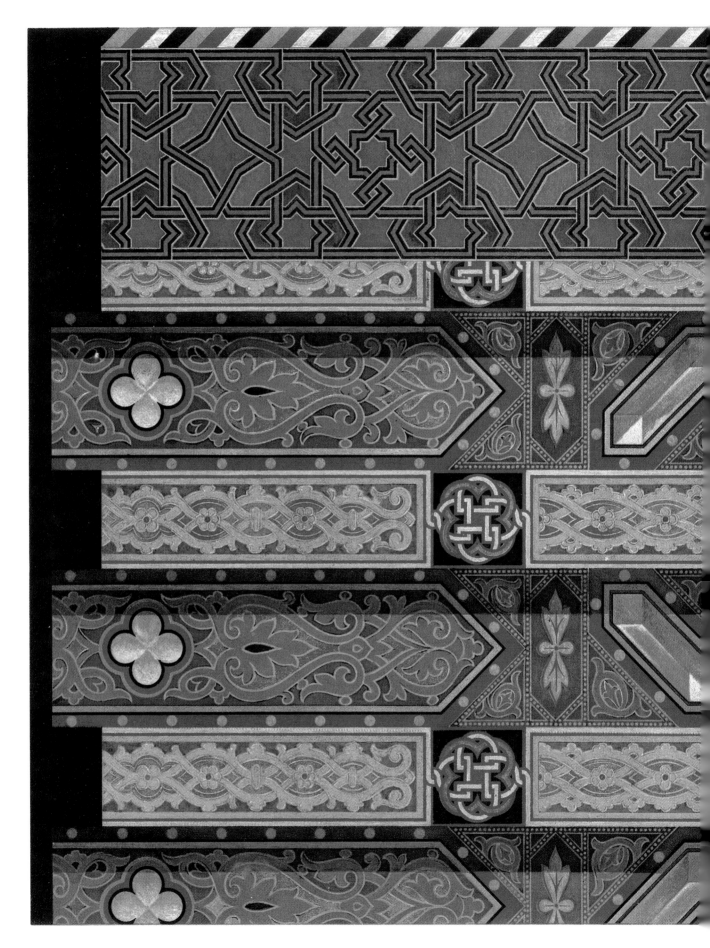

PLATES 50–51. Tunis. Ceiling painting, Bardo Palace, n.d.
[*Farbige Decorationen*]

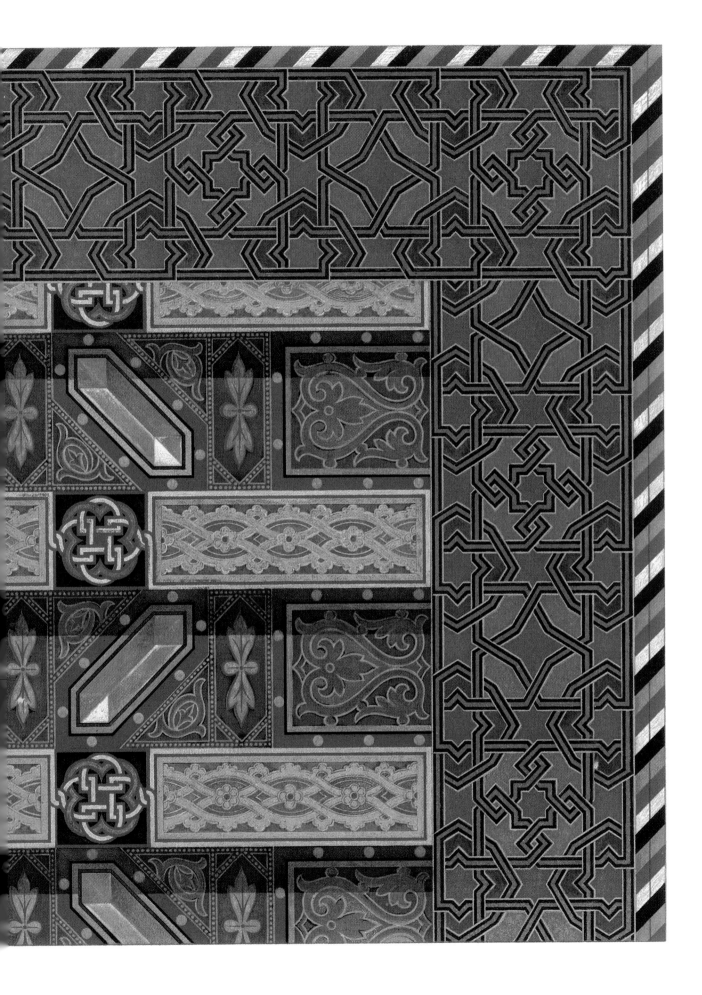

PLATES 52–53. Tunis. Ceiling painting, Bardo Palace, n.d.
[*Farbige Decorationen*]

PLATE 54. Ceiling, Work-room, n.d.
[*La Peinture Décorative en France du xvi au xviii siècle*]

PLATE 55. Beamed ceiling, n.d.
[*La Peinture Décorative en France du xvi au xviii siècle*]

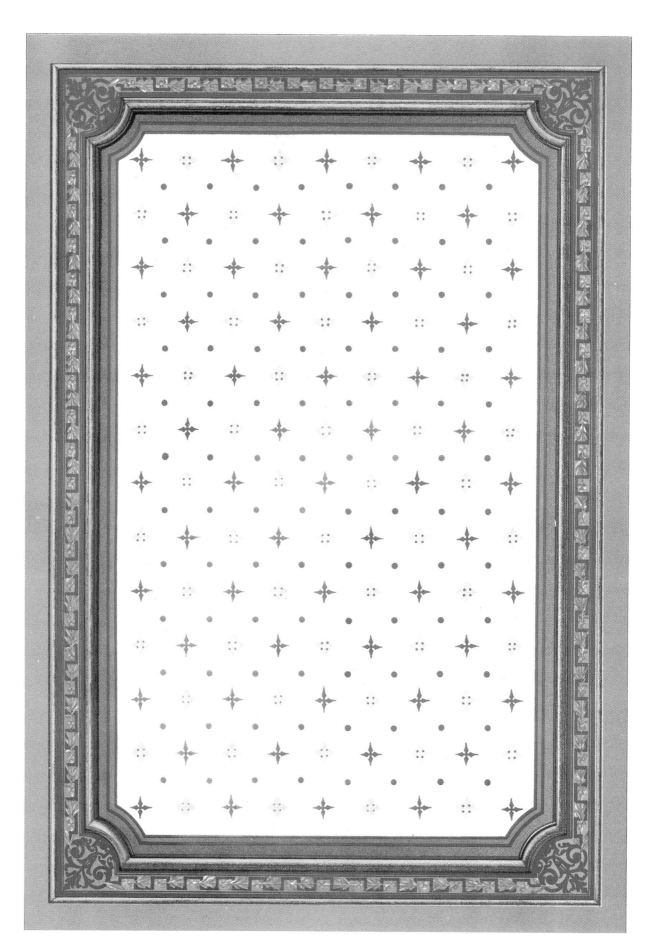

PLATE 56. Bedroom ceiling, n.d.
[*La Peinture Décorative en France du xvi au xviii siècle*]

PLATE 57. Ceiling, Louis XIII, n.d.
[*La Peinture Décorative en France du xvi au xviii siècle*]

PLATE 58. Ceiling, Louis XIV, n.d.
[*La Peinture Décorative en France du xvi au xviii siècle*]

PLATE 59. Ceiling, Louis XIV, n.d.
[*La Peinture Décorative en France du xvi au xviii siècle*]

PLATE 60. Ceiling, Indian motif, n.d.
[*La Peinture Décorative en France du xvi au xviii siècle*]

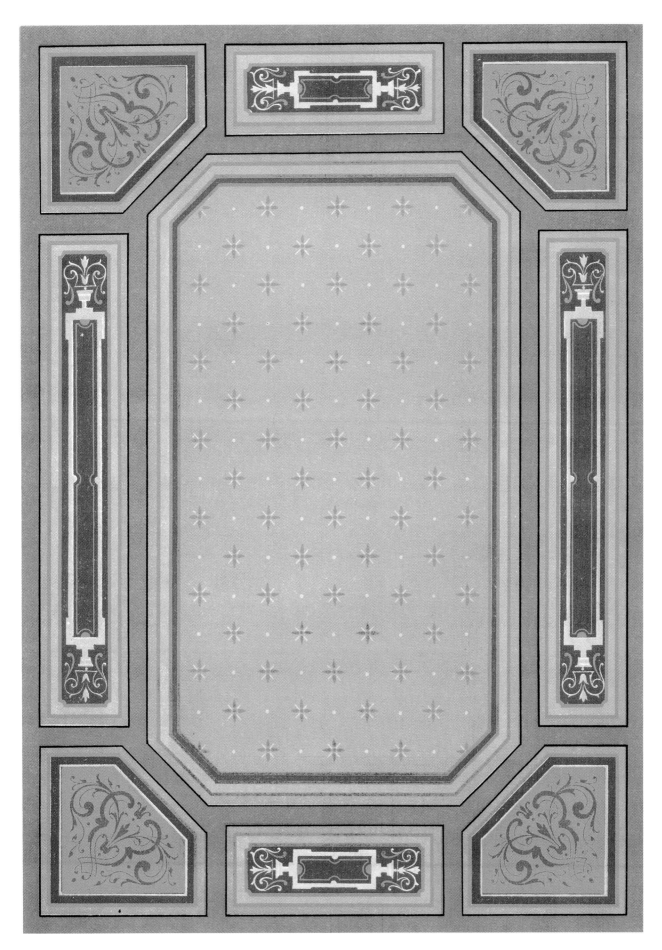

PLATE 61. Ceiling, Henri II, n.d.
[*La Peinture Décorative en France du xvi au xviii siècle*]

PLATE 62. Ceiling, Smoking room, n.d.
[*La Peinture Décorative en France du xvi au xviii siècle*]

PLATE 63. Renaissance ceiling, n.d.
[*La Peinture Décorative en France du xvi au xviii siècle*]

PLATE 64. Renaissance ceiling, n.d.
[*La Peinture Décorative en France du xvi au xviii siècle*]

PLATE 65. Circular ceiling, n.d.
[*La Peinture Décorative en France du xvi au xviii siècle*]

PLATE 66. Drawing-room ceiling, n.d.
[*La Peinture Décorative en France du xvi au xviii siècle*]

PLATE 67. Ceiling, Persian motif, n.d.
[*La Peinture Décorative en France du xvi au xviii siècle*]

PLATE 68. Ceiling, Flight of stairs, n.d.
[*La Peinture Décorative en France du xvi au xviii siècle*]

PLATE 69. Versailles. Ceiling, Music Pavilion, Parc de Petit-Trianon, XVI cent.

[*La Peinture Décorative en France du xvi au xviii siècle*]

PLATE 70. Ceiling, Hotel Dangeau, XVII cent.
[*La Peinture Décorative en France du xvi au xviii siècle*]

PLATE 71. Dining-room ceiling, n.d.
[*La Peinture Décorative en France du xvi au xviii siècle*]

PLATE 72. Rennes, Brittany. Ceiling, Chamber of Parliament, Palace of Justice, n.d.
[*La Peinture Décorative en France du xvi au xviii siècle*]

PLATE 73. Ceiling, Salon des Singes, Chateau de Chantilly, n.d.
[*La Peinture Décorative en France du xvi au xviii siècle*]

PLATE 74. Paris. Ceiling, Hotel de la rue d'Assas, n.d.
[*La Peinture Décorative en France du xvi au xviii siècle*]